From the Central Station to the Mädler Passageway

[1] Central Station

Underground car park at the eastern end
Multi-storey car park at the western end

Leipzig's Central Station is an ideal starting point for a city tour, regardless of whether you arrive by car or by train. The station was inaugurated on 1 October 1915 after 13 years of construction, and is still one of the largest public transport stations worldwide.

Steps over ten yards wide lead to a hall stretching across the whole width of the building; from there, up to 85,000 commuters and travellers daily access the 18 platforms (plus two more in the City Tunnel).

The Bahnhofs-Promenaden, a huge shopping-mall of almost 100,000 sq.ft., was opened in 1997 after two years of construction. It includes over 140 shops, restaurants and bars on two levels and is accessible by escalators and glass lifts.

[2] Nikolaistrasse

On leaving the Central Station by its West Hall and crossing the square, we enter Nikolaistrasse, one of the main shopping streets, and approach the city centre. The street leads to Nikolai Church, St Nikolaus being the patron saint of travellers and merchants.

Till the beginning of the Nazi regime in 1933, the worldwide fur trade was centred in Leipzig, where trading was concentrated at the junction of Nikolaistrasse and Brühl. In recent years the original early-20th-century fur-trading warehouses have been lavishly restored. Animals with fur coats are the decorative motif on most of the tall facades. Wherever a courtyard is open, be sure to take a look inside: still visible today are the storage areas on many levels and the massive wooden beams for holding the cranes used for hoisting the wares.

[3] Old Nikolai School

Leipzig University Antiquities Museum,
Permanent exhibition: The young Richard Wagner
Tue–Thu, Sat, Sun 12–5pm
***Restaurant "Alte Nikolaischule":** opened daily*

Nikolaistrasse leads to Nikolai Churchyard and the massive St. Nikolai Church itself. On the left is Old Nikolai School, founded in 1511, making it the first municipal school not only in Leipzig but in all of Germany. Famous scholars, writers, composers and politicians such as Gottfried Wilhelm Leibniz, Christian Thomasius, Johann Gottfried Seume, Richard Wagner and Karl Liebknecht were educated there.

By 1870 the building had become too small for the growing institution, and so Nikolai School moved to new and larger premises outside the city centre in 1872. Following total refurbishment and rebuilding along historical guidelines from 1991 to 1994, it is now used by the Kulturstiftung Leipzig (Cultural Foundation), the Antiquities Museum of Leipzig University and a restaurant serving local Saxon and international cuisine. Beyond Old Nikolai School we can see the Preacher's House with its turrets and bays; it is in fact the Nikolai Church rectory and was built by Hugo Licht in 1886/87.

Old Nikolai School (left), Preacher's House and Nikolai Column

[4] Nikolai Column

The Nikolai Column standing in front of the rectory is a copy of the columns found inside the church. It was erected as a memorial to the peaceful revolution of 1989, which started right here in St. Nikolai Church and on Nikolai Churchyard. From 1982 on, prayers for peace were being held in the church every Monday. Originally aimed at the nuclear arms race between East and West, they gradually focussed more and more on criticising the political system in the GDR. In the autumn of 1989 the prayer gatherings formed the nucleus of the demonstration marches which have since found their place in German history as the Monday Demonstrations. On the 9 October 1989, calls for "No violence" and "We are the people" on Nikolai Churchyard marked the start of the peaceful revolution, which culminated in the fall of the GDR regime and opened the path to German reunification just one year later. Embedded in the pavement is a bronze plaque with footprints symbolizing these demonstrations, in which up to half a million people took part. The fountain in front of Old Nikolai School was also erected to commemorate the events of autumn 1989.

Karl Liebknecht *1871–1919, politician. Born in Leipzig, the son of Wilhelm Liebknecht, co-founder of the German Democratic Movement, Karl Liebknecht was educated at Nikolai School. In 1914 he was the only member of the German parliament to vote against the issuing of war bonds. In 1918 he and Rosa Luxemburg founded the Communist Party of Germany (KPD). In 1919 he was murdered by officers of the Freikorps ("Free Corps").*

Adam Friedrich Oeser 1717–1799, painter, draughtsman and sculptor. In 1764, Oeser founded the Leipzig Academy of Art (now the Academy of Visual Arts) and remained its director till his death. A friend of Winckelmann, he is considered the most prominent representative of early Neoclassicism in Germany. His most famous pupil was Johann Wolfgang von Goethe. Oeser's paintings influenced public building in the city, including the concert hall of the first Gewandhaus, the Old Theatre, Gohliser Schlösschen and Nikolai Church.*

[5] St. Nikolai Church

Opened daily 10am – 6pm
Guided tours Tue, Thu, Fri 5pm, Sat 11am

St. Nikolai church, built around 1180, is the oldest church in Leipzig. The main entrance on the massive west wing, a relict of the original Romanesque structure, is crested by three towers. The Gothic choir was built about 1400, the north-eastern chapel in the mid-15th century, the south-east chapel around 1567. From 1513 to 1525 the church was rebuilt as a hall church in the late Gothic style. The octagonal central tower, containing the tower guard's apartment, was added by Hieronymus Lotter in 1555. The Baroque pinnacle dates from 1730/31. Between 1785 and 1796, at the initiative of the Lord Mayor, Carl Wilhelm Müller, the interior was completely redesigned in the style of the then innovative and revolutionary classicistic style. Müller found the ideal partner for his ideas in Johann Carl Friedrich Dauthe, a young Leipzig architect. Dauthe clad the late Gothic pillars to produce grooved columns with Egyptian-style capitals ending in a rich array of sprawling palm fronds. The reticulated vaulting became a coffered ceiling, while the choir received a wooden vault lavishly decorated with stucco. The colours white, apple green, gold and old pink symbolise a garden of paradise. Even the pulpit, at the southern corner of the triumphal arch, its sounding roof supported by brass columns, as well as the white benches in the body of the church, harmonize with this theme.

Further victims to this modernisation were the wonderful Renaissance paintings, including works by Lucas Cranach and Georg Lemberger. They are on view today in the Stadtgeschichtliches Museum (Municipal History Museum) and in the Museum der bildenden Künste (Museum of Fine Arts). These "old-fashioned" pictures were replaced by the decorative art of the Leipzig artist Adam Friedrich Oeser, who produced about 30 paintings for the baptismal chapel and the choir, including that over the high altar; influenced by the Enlightenment, they portray the works of Jesus as examples for our daily life. The classicistic baptismal font made of white and gray marble and gilded brass is from 1793. In 1905, four Art Nouveau bas reliefs made of alabaster and illustrating the Way of the Cross were mounted in the choir.

[6] Speck's Hof (Speck's Court)

Opposite the portal of Nikolai Church we can enter the passageway Speck's Hof (Speck's Court), once the largest and most exclusive trade fair complex in Leipzig. This commercial arcade, highly remarkable for its architecture and its passageways, has three entrances; it was constructed in three stages in 1908/09, 1911 and 1928/29. Inside there are three atriums connected to each other by passageways. Of special note is the frieze on the wall of the first atrium. It is made of Meissen porcelain (Dresden china) and shows the structures standing on this site before Speck's Court was built. Leaving the passageway at the Reichsstrasse exit, we look back at the remarkable façade with its beaten copper figures above the ground floor and the natural stone sculptures taken from the world of the Greek gods over the third floor. The brilliant design and the blending of old and new make this passageway one of the most beautiful in Germany.

Passageways
Leipzig is crisscrossed by a network of passageways. This goes back to the open courtyards or open houses of early modern times, complex buildings whose entrances and exits lay on different streets (Barthel's Court). Carts could enter by one and exit by the other without having to turn around. The modern trade fair houses at the turn of the 20th century maintained this tradition (Mädler Passageway, Speck's Court). Nowadays these passageways are commercial buildings and exclusive shopping malls.

[7] Riquet House

Sun–Thu 9am–10pm, Fri, Sat 9am–midnight

Riquet House, standing on the corner opposite Schuhmachergässchen, is particularly eye-catching. It was built in 1908/09 as the trade fair building for Riquet

& Co. Based in Leipzig since 1745, this firm dealt in all types of chocolate products from their own manufacture, as well as in oriental goods, above all tea. This determined the architectural concept of the house: the turret, for example, seems a direct import from China. Other elements are carried out in Art Nouveau. A peacock and a Chinaman are represented in the mosaic high up in the curved gable, while the two elephant heads were the company's trademark. Partly destroyed during the war, the house was restored and reconstructed in 1994/95.

Today it houses a highly recommended Viennese café on the first floor, and on street level a café with a historical flair and an excellent choice of meals and cakes.

[8] Central Trade Fair Palace

At the corner of Grimmaische Strasse and Neumarkt a further trade fair house catches our eye, the Central Trade Fair Palace (Zentralmessepalast), built from 1912 to 1914. The tall stepped gable is reminiscent of older Renaissance buildings in the trade fair's first period of prosperity during the 16th century. The gable is topped by Leipzig's heraldic animal, the lion, with a putto astride. In 1996 the building was gutted for restructuring, leaving only the façade to the present day.

[9] Zeitgeschichtliches Forum (Museum of Contemporary History)

Tue–Fri 9am–6pm, Sat, Sun 10am–6pm
Entrance free of charge

In the 1990s two modern buildings were built next to the Zentralmessepalast, one being the Zeitgeschichtliches Forum. This Museum of Contemporary History is part of the foundation "Haus der Geschichte der Bundesrepublik Deutschland" (House of the History of the German Federal Republic). More than 2500 exhibits illustrate the history of dictatorship and opposition in the GDR.

Positioned across the entrance is a 7.5-ft.-tall figure: the "Jahrhundertschritt" (stride of the century), a bronze sculpture by Wolfgang Mattheuer, representing the two German dictatorships. The sculpture, a symbol for

Wolfgang Mattheuer
1727–2004, painter, graphic artist and sculptor. Mattheuer attended the University of Fine Arts and Book Design in Leipzig and held a professorship there from 1965 to 1974. He subsequently lived in Leipzig as a freelance artist until his death. Together with Bernhard Heisig and Werner Tübke he was the founder of the so-called "Leipziger Schule" (Leipzig school of modern art). He was an important exponent of Critical Realism; his works are classed among the encrypted paintings criticising society in the GDR.

the 20th century, shows a giant aggressively stepping out, his head between his shoulders, one leg booted, an arm stretched for the Hitler salute, the other fist clenched for the communist salute. The second leg is striding out into the future.

[10] Naschmarkt

The square opening up to the right is the Naschmarkt (market for sweet and candies). The building at the end is the Alte Handelsbörse (Old Exchange); in front of this stands the bronze statue of Goethe as a young man.

The market, laid out in 1556, was named from the victuals once traded there. Today's trade fair house Handelshof (Trade Court) stands on the site of the so-called Meat Benches, where butchers offered their wares from the 16th to the 19th century. Sweetmeats and salted fish were also on sale. And, finally, Leipzig's oldest tavern, the Burgkeller, was located here too.

The Lion Fountain at the entrance to the Naschmarkt was a watering place since the middle ages. The two lions were designed by Johann Gottfried Schadow and cast in Lauchhammer in 1820.

[11] Alte Börse (Old Exchange)

Viewing by appointment,
Tel. +49 341 26 17 766

The Old Exchange was built from 1678 to 1687 and functioned as a meeting-place for traders during the fairs. It was Leipzig's first Baroque building. After severe bomb damage in 1943, the façade was reconstructed between 1963 and 1965. Nevertheless, the wonderful interior decorations, the stucco ceiling and its seven paintings have been irretrievably lost. The four figures standing on the roof, Apollo, Mercury, Venus and Athena, are copies of the originals created by Caspar Sandmann in 1683.

Today the Old Exchange building is part of the Leipzig Municipal History Museum and is used for concerts, public lectures and other cultural events.

Portal to the Old Exchange with Leipzig coat of arms

Johann Wolfgang von Goethe
1749–1832, poet and statesman. From 1765 to 1768 Goethe attended the university in Leipzig. The intellectual and cultural life of the city had a lasting influence on him. He visited the theatre, took drawing lessons from Adam Friedrich Oeser, and he and his friends were frequent guests in Auerbach's Cellar. He and Oeser's daughter Friederike became close friends, and he first fell in love in Leipzig, with Käthchen Schönkopf.

[12] Goethe Monument

In front of the Old Exchange stands the Goethe monument made by the sculptor Carl Seffner in 1903. It shows Goethe as a student in Leipzig. Medallions in the plinth show portraits of his two lady-friends in Leipzig: Käthchen Schönkopf, his first love, and Friederike Oeser, the daughter of his revered art teacher, Adam Friedrich Oeser. The monument's location on the Naschmarkt is not coincidental. The sculptor Seffner has Goethe walking with a firm stride towards the Mädler Passage, which, in his time, was the site of Auerbachs Hof (Auerbach's Court) and where the restaurant Auerbachs Keller (Auerbach's Cellar) still exists today. The young student spent many an hour there with his friends, and in his work "Faust" he immortalizes Auerbach's Cellar as an authentic address.

[13] Mädler Passageway

Bistro and restaurant "Kümmel-Apotheke"
Mon–Sat 9.30am–1am, Sun 10.30am–9pm
Tel. + 49 341 96 08 705

Mädler Passageway, the rotunda

The Mädler Passageway forms the node of Leipzig's extensive network of passageways. It was constructed between 1912 and 1914 for the luggage manufacturer Anton Mädler as a trade fair house.

The site had previously been the location of Leipzig's most famous historical trading hall, Auerbach's Court, built between 1530 and 1538 by the physician Dr. Heinrich Stromer von Auerbach. With its 70 vaulted shops selling mainly luxury goods, this house gained renown all over Europe. Not to be overlooked are the two sandstone figures to the right and left of the two-storey entrance: life-sized female figures, one holding a bunch of grapes, the other a vase. These represent the original purpose of the building: it housed a wine-cellar and an exhibition hall for porcelain.

Today the Mädler Passage is Leipzig's noblest shopping mall. It is about 150 yards long and 5 to 7 wide. In the rotunda where the various passages meet, a set of chimes, hung there in 1969 and made of Meissen (Dresden) porcelain, play the popular evening song "Kein schöner Land" (No country more beautiful) every hour on the hour.

Faust and Mephistopheles in front of Auerbach's Cellar

[14] Auerbach's Cellar

Daily 11.30 – midnight
Guided tours regularly Tel. +49 341 216 100

Time for a lunch break. The cuisine of Auerbach's Cellar restaurant is excellent. When it was newly built in 1912, the Luther Cellar, the Goethe Cellar and the famous Wine Cellar one storey lower were preserved in their original late medieval style. As early as 1600 the Leipzig scholar Friedrich Taubmann had declared: "If you come to the Fair in Leipzig and don't go to Auerbach's Court, you haven't been to Leipzig."

Eye-catching at the entrance to Auerbach's Cellar are two groups of bronze figures: Mephistopheles and Faust on one side, scuffling students on the other; both are works by the Leipzig sculptor Mathieu Molitor.

Of all comparable restaurants in Leipzig, Auerbach's Cellar is the one most steeped in tradition. Goethe's drama "Faust" has made it famous worldwide. It was here that Goethe, then 16 years old, heard the story of the ride on the barrel, a tale told and retold for 200 years before his time: Strolling through the busy trade fair, Faust passed a wine-cellar, where several strong men were attempting to carry out a barrel – in vain. Faust mocked them, claiming that one man on his own could manage the task; a fight ensued, whereupon the owner said the barrel would go to whoever could get it out of the cellar without any help. Quickly mounting the barrel like a horse, Faust rode it out of the vault.

Leipziger Allerlei (Leipzig mixed vegetables)

The delicacy Leipziger Allerlei is served seasonally in Auerbach's Cellar and other Leipzig restaurants. It was first mentioned in an 18th century cookery book and is not available all year round because all ingredients must be fresh: baby vegetables that include peas, carrots, asparagus and morels, as well as crayfish. Thus genuine Leipziger Allerlei is served only around May and June, when asparagus is in season, the baby vegetables can be harvested fresh, and crayfish are no longer protected. The dish bears no resemblance whatsoever to the tinned vegetables of the same name.

From Auerbach's Cellar to the Kaffeebaum

[15] The Market Square

The market square covers about 13,000 sq yds and used to be the main trading area. The booths and bustle of the trade fairs had their home here since the 13th century, and it was also the scene of festivities and executions. The last public execution on the market square was that of the murderer Woyzeck in 1824, who later became widely known through Georg Büchner's drama of the same name. A mosaic showing the city's coat of arms marks approximately the site of the executions; stepping on it is considered to bring bad luck. There is an underground station beneath the market. The 2-mile-long City Tunnel joining the Central Station to the Bayerischer Bahnhof (Bavarian Station) has been under construction since 2003 and runs below the entire city centre. The new North-South line joins the south of the city to the dead-end station facing north, ending the situation where trains running south had to circumvent the whole city.

Johann Christian Woyzeck

1780–1824, barber and soldier. On June 2nd, 1821, the obviously confused Woyzeck, driven by jealousy, stabbed his mistress and was condemned to death. He was executed on the market square in Leipzig on August 27th, 1824. The case triggered heated discussions which eventually led to social and psychological factors being taken into account in court. Georg Büchner's drama and Alban Berg's opera have ensured Woyzeck a place in the history of literature and of music.

[16] Old Town Hall

Keystone at the Old Town Hall, Arcade on the corner of Grimmaische Strasse/ Neumarkt

Leipzig Municipal History Museum:
Tue–Sun 10am–6pm. First Wed of every month: entry free of charge. Viewing of the tower and the torture chamber by appointment, Tel. +49 341 96 51 30

The market square is dominated by the most beautiful and famous building in Leipzig, the Old Town Hall. It has been the heart of the town for centuries and without doubt is the finest secular building in Leipzig. Built under the Master Builder and Lord Mayor Hieronymus Lotter in 1556, it manifests the civic self-confidence of a growing commercial centre in the heart of Europe, a confidence justified by many centuries when Leipzig dominated in this function. When the New City Hall was inaugurated in 1905, the former town hall was converted to the town's Municipal History Museum.

Worth seeing is the Great Hall, at one time the finest and largest in Saxony, displaying architectural elements and portraits from the Hall's earliest days to the 19th century. The functions of the Town Hall included not only administration and justice, but also balls and weddings. The visitor should climb up the so-called Pfeiferstuhl (Pipers' Chair), the musicians' gallery over the doorway to the north wing. The impressive display is rounded off by the 16th century open fireplaces and the gallery of portraits of the Electors of Saxony and of the town magistrates. Further attractions in the museum include a detailed model of Leipzig from 1821, showing the town on a scale of 1:380 at around the time of the Battle of Leipzig (Battle of the Nations). Behind the Great Hall is the Ratsstube (Council Chamber), where the aldermen held their consultations; it is still considered Leipzig's most beautiful interior. Going through the the Council Chamber we reach a small side room dedicated exclusively to Johann Sebastian Bach and showing the only existing authentic Bach portrait, painted by Elias Gottlob Haussmann in 1746. (See [26] St. Thomas: Bach biography). On the tower outside, to the left of the portal, a plaque commemorates Robert Blum. Mounted on the occasion of his 100th birthday in 1948, it conceals in the space behind it an urn containing soil from his grave in Vienna. Small shops under the arcades have antiquarian curiosities and Saxon specialities on offer. The only authorized shop selling Meissen (Dresden) china can also be found here.

Robert Blum
1807–1848, writer and politician, grandiloquent orator and representative of the democratic left. In 1832 Blum began working as a secretary in the theatre in Leipzig and founded Germany's first Schiller society in 1840. In 1848 he became a representative for Saxony in the Frankfurt Parliament (the first democratic parliament in German history) on a platform of liberty, democracy and German unity. Despite his parliamentary immunity, Blum was condemned to death by a court-martial in Vienna, and executed by a firing-squad on November 9th, 1848.

Council Chamber, Old Town Hall

[17] Old Weigh-house

Our city tour continues to Katherinenstrasse, named after the chapel of St. Katherina (1420), which was located at the end of the street and demolished in 1544.

At the corner of the market and Katherinenstrasse stands the Old Weigh-house, which housed the municipal weighing scales, thus making it one of Leipzig's most important buildings. All goods brought to Leipzig by merchants had to be weighed and registered here, whereby the fees involved were an important source of income for the city. Customs duties were also levied here. From 1661 to 1712 the building functioned as a post office, but continued to harbour the city council's tap room and wine tavern. In 1917 the newly established Leipzig Fair Office moved in. Destroyed in WW2, the building was rebuilt in 1963/64, although the historical façade was reconstructed only on the side facing the market.

[18] Museum of Fine Arts

Tue, Thu–So 10am–6pm, Wed 12am–8pm

Katharinenstrasse was particularly badly damaged during the Second World War, and most of the magnificent Baroque buildings once lining the right-hand side were destroyed. Today this site is occupied by the new premises of the Museum of Fine Arts.

Founded in 1856/58 by the Leipziger Kunstverein (Leipzig Society of Arts), which itself was established two decades earlier, the museum is one of the oldest civic collections of paintings in Germany. The first building hosting the museum was located at the Augustusplatz (where the Gewandhaus stands today) and fell victim to bombs in 1943. For decades the collection found a provisional home in the former building of the Supreme Court of the German Reich (Dimitrov Museum). The decision in 1992 to relocate the Federal Administrative Court to this building in Leipzig led to plans for a completely new structure for the Fine Arts Museum.

Max Klinger
1857–1920, painter, graphic artist, sculptor. Klinger was one of the greatest exponents of Symbolism. His major works were created in Leipzig: in painting The Judgement of Paris (1886/87), Christ on Mount Olympus (1897), Labour, Wealth and Beauty (1918), and in sculpture The New Salome (1893), Cassandra (1895), and Beethoven (1902). After 1902 Klinger executed numerous marble busts, among them portraits of Franz Liszt, Wilhelm Wundt and Friedrich Nietzsche. In 1916 he founded the Leipzig Annual Exhibition of Fine Arts.

The new complex, designed by the Berlin architects Hufnagel, Pütz, Rafaelian, was inaugurated on December 4th, 2004. On display in the 9000 sq.yds. of exhibition space are paintings from the late middle ages to the present, sculptures of the 19th and 20th centuries and special exhibitions. Its outer shape has led local wits to give the museum the name "Kunstbunker" (Art Shelter). The museum's collection includes numerous works by the Leipzig artist Max Klinger, among them a major example of German sculpture and Klinger's masterpiece: the monumental Beethoven sculpture (1902), showing the musical hero on the throne of the gods. None of Klinger's later works ever attracted as much attention; art historians consider it the epitome of Klinger's legacy.

[19] Frege House

Facing the Museum of Fine Arts is the Frege House (Katharinenstrasse 11), a Baroque merchant's house built in 1706/07. Notable is the double-pitched roof with four banks of dormers, as well as the high vaults at street level which were used by merchants. In 1782 the building was acquired by the financier Christian Gottlob Frege. Inside we find a wide courtyard with a picture embedded in the wall on the left hand side, the so-called Spottbild (Mocking Picture) from 1535. It is a sandstone pedestal which may originally have been part of a window frame, and bears witness to the Reformation: on the left is the pope with his tiara, on the right the German Emperor Charles V (perhaps), or maybe Duke Georg of Saxony; and the monk lying underneath is held to be Martin Luther.

[20] Romanus House

The house at the left-hand corner of Katharinenstrasse and Brühl is the most impressive Baroque building in Leipzig. It was built from 1701 to 1703 by Gregor Fuchs for the Lord Mayor Franz Conrad Romanus. In 1770 it was bought by a wine merchant, Richter, whose café in the seven rooms on the second floor became the centre of social life in the city in the years 1772 to 1794. Friedrich Schiller visited it several times during his stay in 1785. The house was restored in

__Franz Conrad Romanus__ 1671–1746, lawyer. A friend of August the Strong, Elector of Saxony and King of Poland, Romanus was mayor of Leipzig in 1701 and 1703. Under his rule Leipzig became one of the most modern and cleanest towns in Europe: he introduced street lighting by lanterns at night, a sewage system, public waste disposal and paving of the main streets, and also initiated a salary system for the city council. In 1705 he was arrested for forgery and embezzlement, and was held in custody in the fortress of Königstein until his death.

1995. In the corner alcove stands a statue of Mercury, the god of trade, the copy of an original in sandstone from the school of Permoser.

[21] Hainstrasse

Across from the entrance to the Museum of Fine Arts, a passage leads to Hainstrasse, one of the oldest streets in Leipzig. House no. 16–18 is the former Hotel de Pologne, which was used by the Trade Fair Department in the GDR era. From 1843 to 1917 it had experienced better days as a hotel. Restored in accordance with preservation guidelines, the five-storey building harbours an open inner courtyard, three neobaroque banqueting halls and an opulent free-standing marble staircase. After the reconstruction of the historical architecture, the imposing building now houses retail shops and restaurants. The exceptionally attractive banqueting halls can be rented for events. A plate on the house reminds us that, in 1519, Luther stayed in a predecessor building, the residence of the printer Melchior Lotter, during the Leipzig debate.

Hainstrasse 9, on the other side of the street, has been occupied by the Adlerapotheke (Eagle Pharmacy) since 1709. The original house was demolished in 1909 to make place for a new one, which contains the original furnishings of the pharmacy from that time. Theodor Fontane, who later became a famous German novelist, worked there as an assistant from 1841 to 1842.

The Lotter House (Hainstrasse 8), one of the few remaining Renaissance buildings in Leipzig, dates from 1542, when the alderman and merchant Antonius Lotter bought the site. His brother, Hieronymus Lotter, was electoral architect and a later mayor of Leipzig, and the construction of the house is attributed to him. The bay window above all is eye-catching, a richly stuccoed element from the late 17th century (sculptor Johann Jacob Löbelt). In the years 1768 to 1771 this house was occupied by the Russian writer and representative of European enlightenment, Alexander Nikolajewitsch Radistschew, during his academic years at Leipzig University. A little further on (Hainstrasse 5) stands "Kleines Joachimsthal" (Little Joachim Valley), a modern building on the site of the old guesthouse where Friedrich Schiller spent his first weeks in Leipzig and which was destroyed during the Second World War.

Lotter House

Friedrich Schiller
1759–1805, poet and philosopher. Schiller came to Leipzig in April 1785 at the invitation of Christian Gottfried Körner and his friends. In May he and his publisher, Georg Joachim Göschen, moved to a farmhouse in Gohlis (then a small village to the north of Leipzig), where Schiller stayed before following Körner to Dresden in September. During his stay in Leipzig he worked on his drama "Don Carlos" and the "Ode an die Freude" (Ode to Joy). The Schiller house (see p. 46), rediscovered by Robert Blum in 1840, is the oldest memorial site to literature in Germany.

Hainstrasse 3

Gasthaus · Barthels Hof

[22] Barthels Hof (Barthel's Court)

Restaurant "Barthels Hof":
daily 11am – midnight, Tel. +49 341 141 310

Barthels Hof (Barthel's Court) is located on the right, near the market square, at the end of Hainstrasse. Combined with Webers Hof (Court), it is the only surviving court with entrances from two streets. At the time of the trade fairs, these yards worked as mini-markets in themselves.

These commercial premises were constructed between 1747 and 1750 by the architect George Werner for the merchant Gottfried Barthel, and their multipurpose design is still obvious. The vaulted sales rooms and the stables lay on the ground floor, while the upper storeys housed the offices and residential apartments. The attics were fitted out as store rooms; the beams for the cranes used for lifting the goods are still visible.

The oriel window on the court side of the house is a relict from 1523 of an earlier building "Zur goldenen Schlange" (At the Golden Snake), making this the oldest surviving fragment of any private building in Leipzig. The corbel with the golden snake entwining a cross, which gave the house its name, was transferred to the courtyard side of the "new" building in 1750, where it can be admired to the present day. Now as ever Barthel's Court is a business location. The highly recommended restaurant in the inner courtyard, specializing in Saxon cuisine, has been there since 1890.

Theodor Fontane
1819–1898, writer. Follwing an apprenticeship as a chemist, Fontane came to Leipzig in 1841, where he worked as an assistant in the Adler-Apotheke, while at the same time taking his first steps in literature. It was only many years later that he became the most prominent realistic author in Germany. His late works led to the modern German social novel ("Irrungen, Wirrungen", "Frau Jenny Treibel", "Effi Briest", "Der Stechlin".)

[23] Zum Arabischen Kaffeebaum (At the Arabian Coffee Tree)

Restaurant: *daily 11am–midnight*
Tel. +49 341 96 10 060
Coffee museum: *daily 11am –7pm, entry free of charge.*

Passing through Barthel's Court brings us to Barfussgässchen (Bare foot alley), named after the monastery of the Franciscans or Bare Foot Monks located there in the past. Barfussgässchen offers a great variety of restaurants, with tables, chairs and sunshades crowding the pavements in the summer months. To the right the alley opens onto a little plaza with the Lipsia Fountain

Sculpture on the portal of »Zum arabischen Coffe Baum«

(1913), and Kleine Fleischergasse (Little butchers' alley), where the most famous of Leipzig's coffee houses is located, "Zum arabischen Coffe Baum", the oldest coffee "temple" in existence outside the Arabian world. Thirteen different coffee specialities and exquisite home-made cakes are served in the handsome cafés on the first floor or around the fountain outside, allowing us a welcome respite on our tour.

The most obvious feature of the marvellous Baroque building (1718/19) is the sculpture over the entrance, which gave the house its name. A Turk, sprawling under a coffee tree in full flower, his right hand resting on a coffee pot, is handing a cup of coffee to a putto (or vice versa?). Originally this work by an unknown sculptor was highly coloured. Famous regular guests included Gotthold Ephraim Lessing, Richard Wagner, Robert Schumann, Felix Mendelssohn Bartholdy, Robert Blum and Max Klinger. Brass plates set in the wood panelling are engraved with the names of these guests. The Schumann corner in the restaurant is a reminder of the composer, who came here regularly for his wine and discussions on music with the Davidsbündler, the League of David which he had founded and which included a group of young musicians.

__Robert Schumann__ 1810–1856, composer and musical writer. Schumann came to Leipzig in 1828 to study law and took piano lessons with Friedrich Wieck. In 1834 he founded the "Neue Zeitschrift für Musik" (New Journal of Music). In 1840 he married the pianist and composer Clara Wieck. From 1844 on he worked in Dresden and later in Düsseldorf. Schumann was one of the greatest composers of the Romantic Movement. The Schumann family home in Leipzig has been a museum since 2002 (see p. 46).

The house was totally restored in 1998 and now as in the past houses a restaurant with tasty Saxon cuisine, smaller rooms for private meetings, but above all three cafés: the Viennese, the French and the Arabian Café. Most intriguing, however, is the coffee museum in the upper floors, opened in 1999. Spread over 15 rooms we find an overview of the traditions and history of Saxon and European coffee culture in the last 300 years.

MUSEUM COFFE BAUM
AFFEEHAUS
GASTHAUS

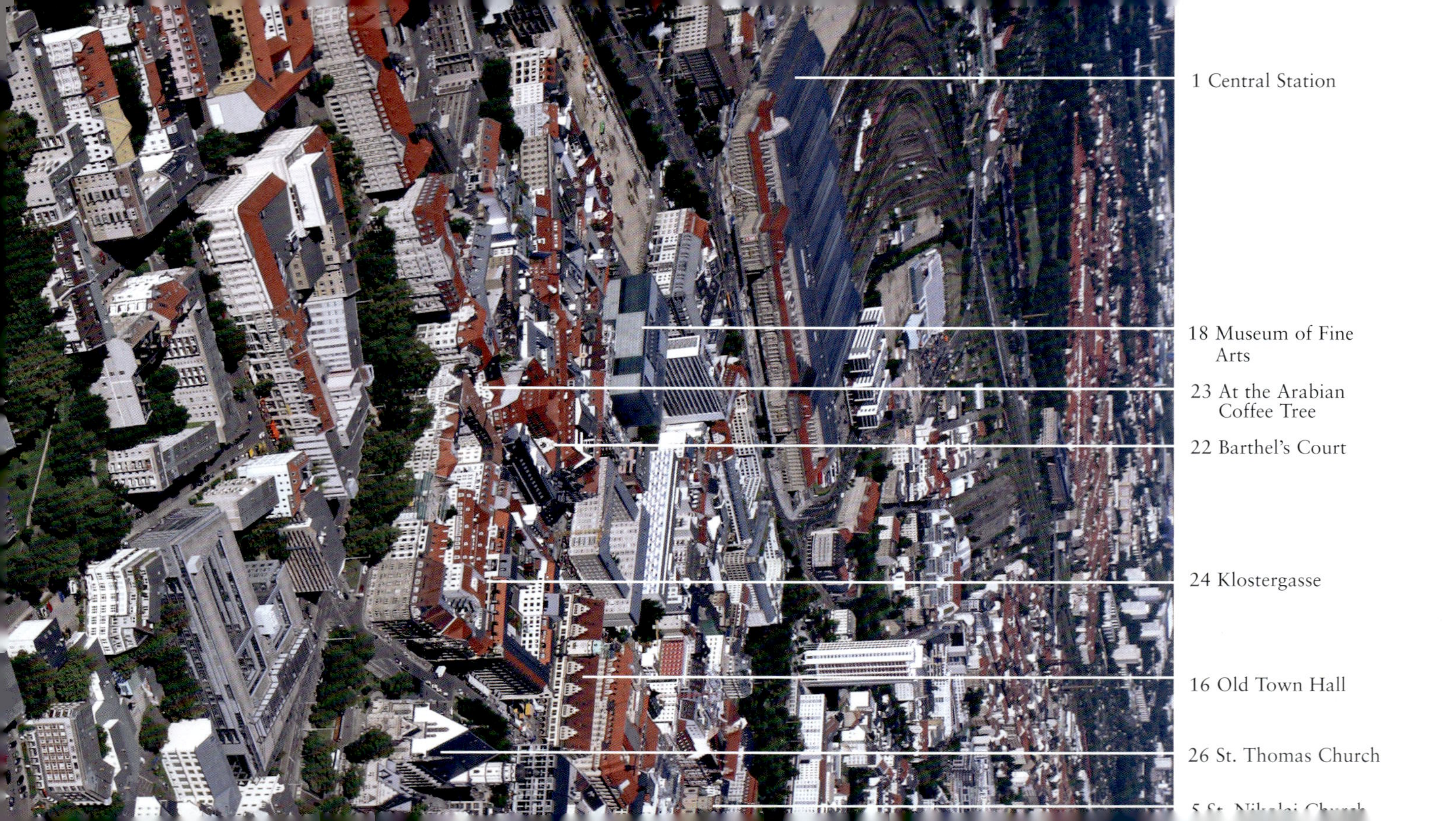
1 Central Station
18 Museum of Fine Arts
23 At the Arabian Coffee Tree
22 Barthel's Court
24 Klostergasse
16 Old Town Hall
26 St. Thomas Church

39 Opera House
37 Augustusplatz
38 University
35 City Store
31 Burgstrasse
33 Petersbogen
43 City Tower
40 Gewandhaus
42 Moritz Bastion
32 New Town Hall

Barfußgässchen

Leipzig skylarks
In the 17th and 18th centuries baked skylarks were considered a culinary speciality. In the second half of the 19th century the hunting of songbirds was prohibited, and in 1876 King Albert I banned the hunting of skylarks in Saxony. There upon some bakers in Leipzig created a pastry similar to the pastries formerly filled with the birds: an oven-fresh shortcrust pastry-case was filled with marzipan, made of almonds and nuts, and a little strawberry jam, and the string with which the birds were trussed crosswise was now made of pastry strips laid across the little cake.

From Barfussgässchen to Augustusplatz

[24] Klostergasse

***Restaurant "Zills Tunnel":** daily 11.30am–midnight*
***"Café Madrid":** Mon–Sat from 11.30am-open end, Sun 10am*

Branching off Barfussgässchen to the right is Klostergasse (Monastery Lane), named after the Monastery of the Augustinian Cannons, St. Thomas, founded in 1212 and formerly located on this site. The corner house on the left is Zills Tunnel, one of Leipzig's historical restaurants, rebuilt in neo-Renaissance style in 1887/88. Very attractive are the three-storey bay, the arched openings on the ground floor and the painting between the windows. The building on the right is the so-called Old Monastery (Klostergsse 5), constructed between 1753 and 1755 by George Werner, with a notable four-winged oaken gate. This also used to be a trade fair building, with space for trading stalls in the ground-floor arches, and storage vaults and stables in the courtyard. The house was later integrated with the adjoining building (Klostergasse 3), which was built in the second half of the 19th century and has housed a restaurant since 1888. The building at the corner of Klostergasse and Thomaskirchhof (St. Thomas Churchyard), today the seat of the Commerzbank, was designed and built as a department store, Ebert, in 1903/04, and represents a harmonious blending of Art Nouveau and neo-Baroque.

Old Monastery and Paulanerpalais

Commerzbank, formerly Kaufhaus Ebert (Topas)

[25] Bach Monument

Beyond St. Thomas Church, on the left, lies St. Thomas Churchyard. In front of the southern portal we see the larger-than-life monument of Johann Sebastian Bach, created by the Leipzig sculptor Carl Seffner in 1908.

Bach is standing in front of an organ, holding a roll of paper in one hand. The left-hand pocket of his coat is hanging inside-out. Perhaps Seffner wanted to show that Bach's pockets were empty, that he never had any money? Or maybe, since his waistcoat is also wrongly buttoned, that for Bach nothing mattered so much as his music, not even his appearance? Nobody knows. The back of the monument depicts in relief Old Thomas School.

[26] St. Thomas Church

Daily 9am–6pm
***Tower tours:** April–Dec, Sat 1pm, 2pm, 4.30pm*
Sun 2pm and 3pm, entry €2
***Choir of St. Thomas:** Motet Fri 6pm,*
with Bach Cantata Sat 3pm, entry €2
Sunday Service 9.30am

St. Thomas Church was built from 1482 to 1496 on the foundations of an older building. Between 1880 and 1889 the church was rebuilt, whereby the entire Baroque interior was removed and replaced by neo-Gothic elements. The plain west façade facing the Promenadenring was redesigned as the main front and a neo-Gothic portal was added. This involved the demolition of Old St. Thomas School, in which Johann Sebastian Bach and his family had lived from 1723 to 1750. Today the Thomas House is located on the site.

Features of special note inside the church are the tombstones with epitaphs from the 15th century in the southern wall, under the stained-glass windows, and at the front of the nave. From right to left the windows depict: Emperor Wilhelm I, Felix Mendelssohn Bartholdy, Martin Luther, Johann Sebastian Bach, Gustav Adolph and the war memorial for the soldiers killed in 1914/1918.

The grave of Johann Sebastian Bach has found its place at the front of the choir since 1950; the simple metal memorial plate (designed by Kunz Nierade) is always strewn with flowers. The marble and alabaster baptismal font in the centre of the choir was created by Franz Döteber in 1614–15. Here, the 12 Bach children born in Leipzig were christened (6 of them died in infancy), and in 1813 Richard Wagner was baptised at this font. The altar in the choir is a late 15th century winged altar. Originally it stood in St. Paul's University Chapel, which was demolished by explosion in 1968 and was set up here in 1984. Visible on the side shown on holy days: eight reliefs from the Jesus –Virgin Mary cycle; the central figure represents St. Paul bearing a book and sword. The Lenten side shows eight paintings from the Passion story. When the wings are closed, two panels depict Paul as a teacher and his decapitation, while the predella shows Paul of Damascus falling from his horse.

***Johann Sebastian Bach** 1685–1750, composer and cantor of St. Thomas. Bach came to Leipzig in 1723 when he succeeded Johann Kuhnau as cantor of St. Thomas and municipal Director Musices. It was here that he wrote his most important works: his major compositions for voice and instruments, works for organ and piano, as well as church music, including the Christmas Oratorio, the St. Matthew and St. John Passions, the Mass in B minor, thirteen piano concertos, more than 300 church cantatas, the Goldberg Variations, the Well-Tempered Clavier. Bach's grave has been in the choir of St. Thomas Church since 1950.*

Karl Straube
1873–1950, organist, choirmaster, cantor of St. Thomas Church. In 1903 Straube became the organist at St. Thomas in Leipzig, and in 1918 he was appointed cantor (until 1938). In 1919 he founded the Institute of Church Music at the conservatory, directing it until 1948. Under his leadership the Choir of St. Thomas had guest performances abroad for the first time in its history, travelling to Denmark and Norway. Straube performed all of Bach's cantatas with the Choir; these were broadcast on the radio, adding immensely to the Choir's popularity. It was while he was cantor that the final rehearsal on Fridays of the motet to be performed in next day's service was opened to the public.

The windows in the choir illustrate the life of Jesus: the adoration of the magi, the baptism of Christ, the resurrection, Christ with the disciples on the road to Emmaus, Christ and Thomas.

The portraits at the sides of the choir represent the superintendents of St. Thomas, beginning top left with the first Lutheran superintendent of Leipzig, Johannis Pfeffinger (in office 1540–1573).

The Sauer organ on the west gallery was installed in 1889. A new organ in the north gallery, inaugurated in the year 2000, is a copy of that in the demolished St. Paul's University Chapel, and allows the authentic sound of Bach's organ music to be reproduced.

The Thomanerchor (Choir of St. Thomas) with its 800-year-old history (founded in 1212) is one of the most famous boys choirs in the world. Integrated in the monastery of the Augustinian canons was a monastery school for the education of new generations of clerics, and from the start liturgical chant formed part of the curriculum. The list of famous cantors is long: Sethus Calvisius (1594–1615), Johann Hermann Schein (1616–1630), Johann Kuhnau (1701–1722), and, most famous of all, Johann Sebastian Bach (1723–1750). Later successors included Johann Adam Hiller (1789–1804), Gottfried Schicht (1810–1832), Karl Straube (1918–1939) and Günther Ramin (1940–1956). Since 1992 the choir has been conducted by Georg Christoph Biller.

As in Bach's day, the motets and cantatas are sung and played in St. Thomas every Friday and Saturday. The choir, together with members of the Gewandhaus Orchestra and the soloists, perform from the west gallery.

[27] Old Bach Monument

A few steps beyond the south portal of the church brings us to the little park on the Ring and the old Bach monument, which is often overlooked not only by tourists but even by locals. The monument, affectionately called the "weather box" by residents of Leipzig, was erected in 1843 on the initiative of Felix Mendelssohn Bartholdy. The work is made of Elbe sandstone and shows a relief portrait of Bach on its northern side.

Felix Mendelssohn Bartholdy
1809–1847, composer and conductor. Mendelssohn, since 1835 conductor of the Gewandhaus orchestra in Leipzig, was responsible for the rediscovery of the music of Bach, which had been practically forgotten. In 1843 he founded the first ever German conservatory in Leipzig (today the University for Music and Theatre). As a composer, conductor, soloist and teacher, Mendelssohn was the outstanding, universally educated European musician of the first half of the 19th century *(see p. 46).*

[28] Mendelssohn Monument

Close to "old Bach", on a 13-foot granite plinth, stands Mendelssohn. The 9-foot-high bronze statue commemorates the man to whom we owe the rediscovery and posthumous canonisation of Johann Sebastian Bach. Seated on the steps at his feet is the Muse of Music, with two angels singing and music-making on either side. On the front of the pedestal stands "Felix Mendelssohn Bartholdy", on the rear "Let the language of music proclaim only what is noble". The sides bear medallions symbolising sacred and secular music. This is a replica of the original bronze monument designed by Werner Stein and unveiled in front of the Second Gewandhaus on Grassistrasse in 1892. In the night of 9 November 1936 the memorial to the "Jew" Mendelssohn had been torn down by the Nazis in a cloak-and-dagger operation, which moved the then Lord Mayor of Leipzig, Carl Goerdeler, to resign. The resurrected statue was unveiled on 18 October 2008.

[29] Bose House

Bach Museum: *Tue-Sun 10am–6pm*

Opposite the southern portal of St. Thomas stands a residential Renaissance house with a fine bay. It is now the home of the Bach Museum.
After entering by the round-arched portal we reach a cross-vaulted lobby with Tuscan columns dating back to the 16th century, when the house was built. From 1709 to 1711 the merchant Georg Heinrich Bose had the house rebuilt in the Baroque style. The result was an attractive ensemble with an inner courtyard and trompe-d'oeil paintings on the façade. Bach, who together with his family was living in Old Thomas School opposite the Bose House, was on friendly terms with the Bose family. The Bach Archive has been located in the Bose House since 1985, alongside a research institute, library and the Bach Museum. In 2010 the house was extensively refurbished and extended, with an exhibition area of about 800 sq. yds. allowing the visitor to learn all about the life and work of Bach and his family, to admire valuable manuscripts, and above all to listen to Bach's music. After a walk through the pleasant little garden, Café Gloria offers you relaxation.

[30] Federal Administrative Court of Germany

Mon–Fri 8am–4pm

The park at the Thomaskirche allows a good view to the south west and the dome of the Federal Administrative Court of Germany. In 1877 the city of Leipzig was selected as the future seat of the Supreme Court of the Reich. Designed by Ludwig Hoffmann and Peter Dybwad and built from 1888 to 1895, the Supreme Court of the Reich was the second major representative structure to be built in the reign of Emperor Wilhelm II. In contrast to the Reichstag building in Berlin, however, the architectural style chosen was not the Baroque but rather the High and Late Italian Renaissance. In commemoration of the Nazi show trial against Georgi Dimitrov and other alleged Reichstag arsonists, the Dimitrov Museum was established here in 1952. In 1992 the German parliament decided to transfer the Federal Administrative Court and the Federal Public Prosecutor to Leipzig. After the stop-gap tenants had all moved out, the building of the former Supreme Court of the Reich was restored for about €100 million and in 2002 the Court was able to move in. The huge entrance hall in the style of a Roman basilica is always open for visitors, as are the wide corridors and the large courtroom.

Reichstag Fire Trial

Fire raged through the Reichstag in Berlin in the night from 27th to 28th February 1933. Despite a massive publicity campaign by the Nazis, the trial they staged in the Leipzig Supreme Court against their Communist adversaries failed to produce the anticipated political triumph. On the contrary: the construed charge had to be dismissed. Georgi Dimitrov's intelligent legal defence proved that the accusations were without any foundation. Only the Dutch anarchist Marinus van der Lubbe, who had also been on trail, was condemned to death.

[31] Burgstrasse

Restaurant "Thüringer Hof": *daily 11am–midnight*

We should turn back to St. Thomas Churchyard. A right turn brings us to Burgstrasse, the former access to the Pleissenburg (castle). In times past, the track from the town hall (today's Old Town Hall) up to the castle of the Saxon electors was arduous: after passing the Vogthof (house of the reeve – it lies beyond the Thüringer Hof), you crossed a wooden bridge over the moat, then came to a drawbridge and three gates, each secured with a portcullis, before finally reaching the yard of the castle.

The inn Thüringer Hof (Thuringian Court) located in Burgstrasse 19–23 has been open since 1838. Badly damaged in the war, it was completely demolished in 1994, reconstructed on historical lines, and reopened in 1996 serving "genuine Thuringian cuisine".

Martin Luther
1483–1546, theologian and reformer. With his 95 theses in 1517, Luther protested against the practice of indulgences and queried papal infallibility. In the Leipzig debate in the Pleissenburg in 1519 he denied the infallibility of the church. He was excommunicated, proscribed by the papal bull and the imperial ban, and fled to the Wartburg (castle), where he proceeded to translate the New Testament into German. It was only after the death of Duke Georg of Saxony in 1539 that the Reformation was brought to Leipzig – on May 25th, 1539, Luther himself delivered the reformation sermon in the Church of St. Thomas.

[32] New Town Hall

Restaurant "Ratskeller":
Mon–Sat 11am–11pm
Sun & holidays: 11am–3.30pm

Burgstrasse leads us directly to the New Town Hall, one of the most significant German town halls built at the turn of the century. Constructed between 1899 and 1905 according to plans drawn up by the director of the municipal Office of Works, Hugo Licht, it has been the seat of the Leipzig City Council since 1905. Since medieval times it had been the site of the Pleissenburg, where the Leipzig debate between Luther and Eck took place in 1519. The New Town Hall covers an area of more than 13,000 sq yds and contains about 600 rooms. The words in the gable over the entrance, "Arx nova surrexit" (A new castle has arisen), symbolise the self-confidence of an ambitious city.

With an altitude of almost 149 metres, the tower is listed in the Guinness book of records as the highest tower of any town hall in the world. The Latin inscription under the clock says "Mors certa, hora incerta" (Death is certain, its hour uncertain). The locals have their own translation: "It's a dead cert the clock is wrong."

[33] Petersbogen Passageway

Going through the Petersbogen Passageway, built in 2001, we reach Petersstrasse. In times past, this was the site of the Collegium Juridicum, the former Law School of Leipzig University. The older building was rebuilt in 1882 with a passage to the Schlossgasse (Castle Alley), but was destroyed in World War 2. The gap between the remaining buildings was filled with the present passage, which contains a rotunda, lifts and escalators, and hosts shops, the Law School of the university as well as its library, a cinema, restaurants and a casino.

[34] Petersstrasse

Petersstrasse has always been one of the liveliest shopping streets in the city centre. With the trade fair houses Messehof (Trade fair court), Petershof (Peter's Court), Drei Könige (Three Kings), Stentzlers Hof (Stenzler's Court), and the huge new department stores of recent years, it is now Leipzig's no. 1 shopping street. There are few remnants in the street of the original Baroque housing. One exception is house

Trade Fairs
Documentary evidence for trade fairs in Leipzig dates back to the 12th century. Lying conveniently at the junction of the Via Regia (leading from the Rhineland to Eastern Europe) and Via Imperii (from Italy to the Baltic Sea), Leipzig's geographic position facilitated long-distance trade. In 1497 Emperor Maximilian I upgraded the normal fairs to imperial trade fairs, enabling Leipzig to develop into one of the most important trading centres in Europe. 1895 saw the evolution from a trading fair to an exhibition centre where only samples were shown, the first of its kind in the world. In 1996 the new show grounds were opened in the north of the city.

no. 24, with its emblem of an Eskimo in his kayak, which gave the house its name "Der Grönländer" (the Greenlander). The tradition associated with this sumptuous Baroque building and its fine bay (built from 1744 to 1751 by George Werner) relates that a descendant of the former owner, Johann Martin Haugk, was shipwrecked while seal-hunting in the polar sea and was rescued by an Eskimo (called Greenlander). The emblem is said to have been affixed in memory of this event in 1875. In the restoration of the interior of the house in 1994 only the Baroque stairwell and the vaults at the rear were kept; the inner courtyard was roofed over with glass. Today a shop for footwear and offices are located here.

Petersstrasse and Neumarkt are connected by the Messehof (Trade Fair Court) Passageway. This shopping passageway is more than 108 yards long, and we leave it at the Neumarkt, named after the "new" Leipzig market in 1390.

[35] City Department Store

The building facing us when leaving the Messehof Passageway has a significant place in cultural history. The City Department Store (Städtisches Kaufhaus), built between 1893 and 1901, was the first sample exhibition house in the world (in contrast to selling

the goods in situ). Before that date this had been the site of the cloth-manufacturers' house, the Gewandhaus (Cloth Hall), with Leipzig's first concert hall located on its first floor (built in 1781 by Dauthe). This is the origin of the name by which the orchestra and its concert hall are still known today.

At the rear of the building, in Universitätsstrasse, the 7-ft.-tall bronze statue of Emperor Maximilian I can be admired on the façade above the portal. In 1497 Maximilian conferred the first imperial trade fair charter on Leipzig, thereby raising the status of the city's trade fair to that of a fair in the Holy Roman Empire.

Just a few steps beyond the City Department Store, a plaque on the wall of the store Galeria Kaufhof reminds us that this was the former location of an opulent Baroque building known as the "Grosse Feuerkugel" (The Huge Fireball), destroyed in 1943. We read that the famous German writers Gotthold Ephraim Lessing and Johann Wolfgang Goethe lived in this house during their academic years in Leipzig in 1755–1757 and 1765–1768 respectively.

Bay of the Fürstenhaus

[36] Grimmaische Strasse

Grimmaische Strasse goes east towards Grimma and Dresden. After 1421 the street used to end at the Grimmaische Tor (City Gate). This was a relict of the old city wall and was demolished in 1835, as it proved to be a hindrance for the trade fair traffic.

On house no. 17, a new building from 1986, an unusual bay catches our eye. The bay is a copy – the original was part of the Fürstenhaus (the Princes' House), which stood opposite until destroyed in the Second World War. The Fürstenhaus was built in 1558 by reconstructing a previous dwelling, parts of which have been preserved. At the corners towards Grimmaische Strasse it had two round bays, built by the master bricklayer Paul Widemann. The name "Fürstenhaus", certifiable since 1618, goes back to 1612, when four princes from Altenburg stayed in the house.

On April 1, 1828, Anton Philipp Reclam opened a lending library with a reading room, the Literarisches Museum (Museum for Literature) in this street. Later he started Reclams Universal-Bibliothek, the oldest paperback series that is still in existence.

Anton Philipp Reclam *1807–1896, publisher. On October 1, 1828, Reclam founded a publishing company in Grimmaische Strasse. Later he enlarged it by purchasing a printing works. From November 1867 on he published inexpensive editions of German and world literature under the title of "Reclams Universal-Bibliothek" – up to 5000 titles by the time of his death. In 1887 Reclam began with the construction of a new publishing works at Inselstrasse 22, which was completed only in 1905.*

[37] Augustusplatz

The inscription above the clock on the Kroch high rise says "Omnia vincti labor" – work overcomes everything.

Grimmaische Strasse opens onto Augustusplatz, whose ca 45,000 sq. yds. make it the largest square of any German city. Architecturally it also used to be one of the most beautiful in the country, but suffered particularly severe damage in the war. During the GDR era the gaps were closed; the Central Post Office on the eastern side is now under a preservation order. The only buildings to survive were those on the north-western side, of which the Kroch Tower Building (1929), the first Leipzig high-rise, is worth mentioning. The huge bell-men on the roof swing their hammers every fifteen minutes to mark the quarter hour.

Augustusplatz is also remembered as the place where the demonstrators assembled after the Monday demonstrations in 1989. Today's design with the exits and ventilation openings ("milk pots") of the underground car-park is the subject of controversy.

After the Central Station Square, Augustusplatz is Leipzig's most important tram intersection.

[38] University

All the buildings located at the corner of Grimmaische Strasse and Augustusplatz are part of the university. Founded in 1409, it is the second oldest German university in existence. Many famous personalities have been educated and have worked there: Leibniz, Thomasius, Gottsched, Lessing, Klopstock, Gellert, Goethe, Wundt, Fechner, Heisenberg, Mayer, Bloch to name but a few.

Until 1968 the Church of St. Paul, a Late Gothic monastery church, was located beside the Augusteum, the neoclassical main building of the university. After the dissolution of the monasteries in 1544 it became the university church. Undamaged during the war, in May 1968 it was blown up at the command of Walter Ulbricht, Head of State of the GDR at the time. With this, one of Leipzig's most valuable buildings, with a unique architectural and cultural history, was irretrievably destroyed. Even the Augusteum, damaged in the war, was demolished as a relict of "bourgeois culture". It was replaced (1968–72) by the new university with the university tower building. Since then the tower has found a new use (see p. 44). With the 800th anniversary of the university in view, the GDR structures have been replaced by a new campus. The centrepiece is the Paulinum – an assembly-hall and university chapel St Pauli, designed by the architects van Egeraat, Rotterdam. The inauguration is in 2014.

Werner Heisenberg
1901–1976, physicist. In 1927 at the age of 26 Heisenberg was made a professor at Leipzig University. Prior to this he had worked with Niels Bohr in Copenhagen and together with Max Born and Pascual Jordan had established quantum mechanics. For this he received the Nobel Prize for Physics in 1932 and the Max Planck medal in 1933. Because of his research in the uranium project and the atomic bomb in the German army ordnance office during the Second World War he was interned until 1946. Later he directed the Max Planck Institute for Physics in Munich till 1970.

Richard Wagner
1813–1883, playwright and composer. Born in Leipzig in 1813, Wagner attended school (1817–1822, 1828–1830) and university (1831–1833) here. His operas were neglected by the people of his home town for a long time – the first Leipzig performance of one of his operas, "Tannhäuser" was staged only in 1853. In 1862 he conducted the orchestra himself for the first time in a special concert in the Gewandhaus. Wagner was continually besieged by creditors until, in 1864, King Ludwig II of Bavaria provided him with a guaranteed income.

[39] Opera House

Facing the Kroch House is the Opera House, a new building dating from 1956 to 1960 and the first newly built theatre in the GDR. The site, next to the Swan Pond, a remnant of the ancient city moat, was the location of the neoclassical New Theatre (1868), which was severely damaged by British bombs in 1943. The Opera House is a neoclassical structure which sets standards and is now listed for preservation. Peace doves form the decorative motif along the 370-yard-long attic balustrade. The auditorium seats 1250. One of the most prestigious orchestras in the world, the Gewandhausorchester, has its place in the orchestra pit, while the ballet company is in international demand.

The Leipzig Opera has a very long tradition. It was founded in 1693 (only the Hamburg Opera is older), and with musicians like Georg Philipp Telemann and Johann Adam Hiller soon gained fame far beyond the borders of the city. In 1878 Richard Wagner's Ring cycle was staged here in full, the first performances outside Bayreuth.

[40] Gewandhaus

Stairwell

The New Gewandhaus (in fact the third) is located on the southern side of the Augustusplatz. Opened in 1981, it is the only concert hall built in the GDR (architect Rudolf Skoda). The first hall (1781) was demolished in favour of a trade fair house in 1885 (see [34] City Store), while the second building in Beethovenstrasse fell victim to American bombardment in 1944. For 35 years the orchestra played in temporary accommodation (the Capitol Cinema or the Congress Hall in the zoo).

With its huge glass façade, the modern concert hall allows visitors outside to see the interior, and when concerts are playing the lighting inside allows the large painting (930 sq.yds.) by Sighard Gille to reach its maximum effect. The Grand Concert Hall with 1920 seats is reminiscent of an antique amphitheatre. The organ was built by the organ building firm Schuke and is the largest musical instrument ever built in the GDR. It contains 6638 pipes and 89 stops, the organ façade is 11 yards high and 16 wide. The inscription above the organ reads "Res severa verum gaudium" ("True joy is a serious matter", Seneca), the motto ever since the concerts began.

Kurt Masur
Born 1927, conductor. For a quarter of a century Kurt Masur determined the musical life of the city. In 1970 he succeeded Vaclav Neumann as conductor of the Gewandhaus Orchestra. His credo was to maintain the great tradition of the orchestra while simultaneously promoting what was new. Under his baton the orchestra, with its rich tradition, gained even more international acknowledgement, undertaking 900 tours in the 26 years of his leadership. Masur was a member of the "Leipziger Sechs" (Leipzig Six), and at the Monday demonstration of October 9, 1989, he called for calm and reflected action, demanded open discussions and played a major role in preventing the situation getting out of hand and peaceful demonstrators being shot at. In 1989 he was made an honorary citizen of Leipzig.

Contemporary artists produced large-scale paintings for the foyers. The small concert hall (chamber music and events) has seating for 500 listeners.

The Leipzig Gewandhaus Orchestra was founded in 1743 as "Grosses Konzert" (Grand Concert), making it the oldest civic orchestra in the world. It is also the largest; the musicians have always played not only in the Gewandhaus (48 symphony concerts, 12 chamber music evenings and 20 special concerts annually), but also for the opera, and they accompany the Choir in St. Thomas Church. A section of the orchestra is often on tour. The famous Gewandhaus conductors include, among others, Felix Mendelssohn Bartholdy (1835–1847), Arthur Nikisch (1895–1922), Wilhelm Furtwängler (1922–1928), Franz Kowitschny (1949–1962), Kurt Masur (1970–1996), Herbert Blomstedt (1998–2005). Since 2005, the prestigious orchestra has been conducted by Riccardo Chailly.

[41] Mende Fountain

The Mende Fountain in front of the Gewandhaus was inaugurated in 1886. In the form of an allegory, in which all types of aquatic creatures and figures from Greek mythology are romping about, it illustrates the importance of water to man.

Associated with the fountain is an ineradicable legend: the donor, Marianne Pauline Mende, widow of a Leipzig merchant, is said to have run an establishment of dubious repute and to have tried to atone for her sins with this donation. Thus wrote the famous reporter Egon Erwin Kisch. He was taken in by a mistaken identity, a fact which refuses to gain wider public acceptance.

[42] Moritz Bastion

Events: *Tickets Tel. +49 341 702 590*
"Café Barbakane": *Mon–Fri 10am–open end, Sat. noon–open end, Sun brunch from 9am*
Tel. +49 341 70 25 930

Passing to the right of the Gewandhaus, we reach the Moritz Bastion (Moritzbastei). It is the last remaining relict of the medieval and early modern city fortifica-

mdr

tion, built at the behest of Elector Moritz from 1551 to 1553 by the electoral architect and subsequent Mayor of Leipzig, Hieronymus Lotter.

Today the remaining vaults and casemates are used by the student club "mb", the largest student club in Europe, containing restaurants and cafés. The students themselves began to excavate the buried vaults of the barbican in 1974. A total of 30,000 young people worked for about 150,000 unpaid hours and removed 40,000 cubic yards of debris. At the side of the bastion facing away from the city we can still see the electoral-Saxon coat of arms with the year "1551" on the weathered sandstone.

The monument for Albrecht Thaer (1752–1828) was reerected at the main entrance to the Bastei in 2011. Thaer founded the science of agriculture, and developed the first agricultural teaching institute as well as the first agricultural academy in Germany. The monument was created in 1850 by Ernst Rietschel, one of the leading German sculptors of the late neoclassical period, and stood at the Moritz Bastion till 1947. Placed in front of a university institute after the war, it has returned to its original site after 64 years.

[43] City Tower

Restaurant "Tower – Plate of Art":
Mon – Thu 11am – midnight,
Fri/Sat 11am – 1am, Sun 9am – 11pm

The City Tower, built in 1968 – 1972 (architect Hermann Henselmann) used to be part of the university. It is 151 yds tall and was listed for preservation in the year 2000. The new two-storey annex to the tower (2001, architect Peter Kulka) houses rehearsal halls for the symphony orchestra and the radio and children's choirs of the Mitteldeutscher Rundfunk (mdr-Central German Broadcasting Company). It is connected to the Gewandhaus by a 24-yard-long bridge 6.5 yards above the ground.

A visit to the restaurant and café on the 27th floor is an absolute must; it provides a fascinating view of the city. One storey higher there is an open platform which gives an overwhelming view across the whole of Leipzig and far out into the regions beyond.

[44] Völkerschlachtdenkmal (Monument of the Battle of Leipzig / Battle of the Nations)

Daily 10am – 6pm, Nov.–Mar. 10am–4pm

Leipzig's landmark on Prager Strasse can only be reached by transport, either by car (car parks available) or by tram No. 15 from Augustusplatz (bound for Meusdorf).

The monument was erected to commemorate the Battle of Leipzig (16th–19th October 1813). In the biggest mass battle of the 19th century, Napoleon's army was decisively defeated by the allied armies of Prussia, Russia and Austria. Half a million soldiers took part, and every fifth one was killed, in addition to 10,000 wounded. The villages surrounding Leipzig were devastated.

The construction of the monument was at the initiative of the Leipzig architect Clemens Thieme, who founded the Deutscher Patriotenbund (German League of Patriots) to finance the project. The monument, which cost 6 million gold marks and was designed by Bruno Schmitz (Kyffhäuser monument, Porta Westfalica, Deutsches Eck) took 15 years to complete and was inaugurated on October 18, 1913. At 96 yards high, it is the most massive monument in Europe.

Napoleon Bonaparte *1769–1821, Emperor of France. Napoleon ended the French Revolution with the overthrow of the Directory in 1799. He was named First Consul and had himself acclaimed Napoleon I, Emperor of the French, in 1804. His reforms at home created a unified system of administration; the Civil Law Code (Code Napoleon) produced under his rule became the standard in many parts of Europe. By means of successive wars he attempted to impose his hegemony in Europe, in which he was successful until the Russian campaign of 1812. He was defeated by the allied armies in the Battle of Leipzig (Battle of the Nations) and died in exile on the island of St. Helena.*

Krypta

Recommendations

Mendelssohn House

Goldschmidtstrasse 12, Tel. +49 341 12 70 294
Daily 10am–6pm, Concerts every Sun at 11am

The former apartment of the Mendelssohn family in the late neoclassical building of 1844, the last authentic and only existing private address, is exquisitely furnished with original furniture, objects of art, and hand-written documents belonging to the family.

Schumann House

Inselstrasse 18, Tel. +49 341 39 39 620,
Wed–Fri 2pm–5pm, Sat / Sun 10am–5pm
(and by arrangement)

After their wedding Robert and Clara Schumann moved into the newly built neoclassical house in 1840. It was here that Schumann composed among others the Frühlings-(Spring) symphony, and two of his children were born. Besides the exhibition there is an elementary school with a strong artistic stream in the house.

Schiller House

Menckestrasse 42, Tel. +49 341 56 62 170
April–Oct.: Tue–Sun 10am–6pm
Nov.–Mar.: Wed–Sun 10am–4pm,
guided tours Wed 5pm

The house, built in 1717, is the oldest existing farmhouse in Leipzig. Friedrich Schiller lived here during his stay in the city in the summer of 1785. Today it is the oldest literature memorial in Germany and contains original and unusual objects associated with the poet.

Museum in the "Runde Ecke" (Round Corner)

Dittrichring 24, Tel +49 341 96 12 443
Daily 10am–6pm, entry free of charge

The district administration of the Staatssicherheit ("State Security" – Stasi) was occupied by civil rights campaigners on December 4, 1989. Today it is a memorial site with unique evidence about and objects from the activities of the Secret Service of the GDR.

Alte Spinnerei (Old Spinning Company)

Spinnereistrasse 7, Tel +49 341 49 80 270

The cotton spinning mill, founded in 1884, was once the largest spinning mill in continental Europe. Since 1992 the industrial wasteland has been populated by artists and has become an internationally respected, creative art centre. Graphic artists ("New Leipzig School"), architects, designers, trendsetters etc. live and work here. It is home to eleven galleries, some with a world-wide reputation (Eigen+Art).

Russian Church

Russian Orthodox Church (Moscow Patriarchate)
Philipp-Rosenthal-Strasse 51a, Tel +49 341 87 81 453
Summer: daily 10am–1pm/2pm–5pm
Winter: daily 10am–1pm/2pm–4pm
The church was built in 1913 in commemoration of the 130,000 Russians who fought against the army of Napoleon in 1813, and especially of the 22,000 Russian soldiers killed in action. Of special note is the 18-yd.-high wall of icons, of which there are over 70 on view.

German Book and Writing Museum of the German National Library

Deutscher Platz 1, Tel +49 341 22 71 324
Tue–Sat 10am–6pm, Thu 10am–8pm
Founded in 1884 as the German Book Trade Museum, since 1950 a section of the German National Library, it is the world's oldest book museum. The valuable exhibits cover all ages and cultures.

Zoological Garden

Pfaffendorfer Strasse 29, Tel +49 341 59 33 385
Nov.–Mar. 9am–5pm
Apr., Oct. 9am–6pm, May–Sept.: 9am–7pm
Wide variety of catering facilities
Founded in 1878, Leipzig Zoo is one of the oldest, and with its 900 different species, one of the most diverse in the world. Every year more than 1.7 million visitors walk through the park with its 48 acres and marvel at the approx. 6600 animals living there. Since 2011 visitors can also see animals from the tropical rainforests in Godwanaland.

Grassi Museum

Johannisplatz 5–11
Tue–Sun 10am–6pm
The Grassi Museum, built between 1925 and 1929, houses three important museums of national and international repute:

- *Museum of Applied Art, Tel +49 341 22 29 100*
  European and non-European arts and crafts, textiles, ceramics and porcelain, furniture and glass, metal wares.
- *Museum of Ethnography, Tel +49 341 97 31 900*
  Part of the State Ethnographic Collections of Saxony, exhibits of peoples and cultures from all parts of the world.
- *Museum of Musical Instruments, Tel + 49 341 97 30 759*
  Part of the University of Leipzig, largest collection of musical instruments in the world.

Leipzig in One Day. A City Tour
4th English Edition (revised) 2013

Text: Doris Mundus
Translation: Jutta Rosen-Schinz
Map: Peer-Cedric Hänsel
Photo credits: Torsten Pape, exceptions: Hans-Dieter Kluge (14, 15t, 22, 23, C6), Peer-Cedric Hänsel (16b), Punctum / Peter Franke (5, 9b, 19t, 19b, 20, 26b, 27tl, 36), Punctum / Stefan Hoyer (15b), Punctum / Bertram Kober (10, 24/25, 31, 44), Punctum/Hans-Peter Szyszka (28, 35t, C2), Punctum (12b, 35b, 45b), Publisher's archive (32, 39, 47, C5)
Design, layout: Gabine Heinze, TOUMAart
Production: Bosch-Druck GmbH, Ergolding

Cover:
1 Old Town Hall
2 St. Nikolai Church
3 St. Nikolai Church, column
4 Old City Hall, detail
5 Trade fair on the Market Square in 1825

www.lehmstedt.de

ISBN 978-3-937146-53-9